Dolphins:100 An
Pictures

By Bandana Ojha

All Rights Reserved ©2018

Introduction

Filled with up-to-date information, color photos, fascinating & fun facts this book " ***Dolphins:100 Amazing Facts with Pictures*** " is the best book for kids to find out more about the amazing creature Dolphins. This book would satisfy the children's curiosity and help them to understand why dolphins are special—and what makes them different from other animals. The book gives a story, history, detailed science, explores the interesting facts about largest orca dolphins, smallest Maui's dolphins, most popular bottlenose dolphins and their place in the world. This is a great chance for every kid to expand their knowledge about dolphins and impress family and friends with all discovered and **never** known before fun filled facts.

1. Compared to other animals, dolphins are believed to be very intelligent. It is believed by scientists that comparing the ratio size of brain to body, dolphins take the 2nd place right after the humans.

2. Dolphins are better swimmers than fish and this is because they carry loads more oxygen in their blood than fish, which helps them to swim longer than a fish.

3. Dolphins often display a playful attitude which makes them popular in human culture. They can be seen jumping out of the water, riding waves, play fighting and occasionally interacting with humans swimming in the water. Dolphins are sometimes thought of as the dogs of the sea because they are usually playful and friendly.

4. There are 36 species of dolphins,32 types of ocean dolphins,4 types of river dolphins.

5. Female dolphins are called cows, males are bulls and young dolphins are called calves. Just like cow family.

6. The dolphin is the only mammal that gives birth with the tail first instead of the head, and this is to make sure their baby doesn't drown.

7. A mother dolphin provides very rich milk for her calf for at least one year and usually longer. A calf has a specially adapted tongue allowing it to form a straw shape for ingesting the milk without ingesting any salt water. Babies stay with their mothers until they can search for food on their own. They stay with their moms for about 2 to 3 years.

8. Dolphins never fully fall asleep. Only one side of a dolphin's brain sleeps at a time. Part of their brain always stays awake, so they can breathe.

9. Dolphins live in a group called a school or pod.

10. Dolphins use squeaks and whistles to call and chat each other.

11. Dolphins can swim 25 *mph* miles per hour.

12. Some dolphins can jump as high as 30 ft out of the water.

13. They have good eyesight and great hearing. Dolphins can hear better than humans.

14. An Atlantic bottlenose dolphin has 80 - 100 cone-shaped teeth which they use for trapping

their prey. Dolphins never chew their food, they swallow it. Their teeth are used only to catch their prey.

15. A baby dolphin (calf) is born with whiskers on its upper jaw (rostrum) which fall out soon after birth.

16. Dolphins eyes produce tears that protects their eyes from foreign objects and infection as well as reducing the friction between their eyes and the sea water.

17. A dolphin's skin is very sensitive and delicate and can be easily damaged.

18. Dolphins shed their skins, just like snakes, it helps to get rid of algae and bacteria that can cling to their skins.

19. Dolphins cannot breathe under water. They breathe from a blowhole at the top of their heads.

20. Orca is the largest species of dolphins. Orcas can be 25ft long and 19,000 pounds. Even though it is sometimes called a killer whale, it is in fact a member of the dolphin family.

21. Orca are effective hunters. They prey on seals, sea lions, fish, sea birds, turtles, octopuses, and squid. Orcas will even attack other whales, including the enormous blue whale which can measure over three times their size.

22. Maui Dolphin is the smallest species of dolphins. They are about 4ft long and 90 pounds.

23. Fish normally swim with their tails moving from side to side, but dolphins swim by moving their tails up and down.

24. Dolphins love their pod family; they've often been seen caring for the sick and the elderly as well as injured dolphins.

25. Scientists believe that dolphins conserve energy by swimming alongside ships, a practice known as bow-riding.

26.When humans take a breath, they replace only 15% of the air in their lungs with fresh air. When dolphins take a breath, they replace 90% of the air in their lungs with fresh air.

27. Bottlenose dolphins are the most common and well-known type of dolphin. They are usually gray in color.

28. It has been researched that dolphins are "re-entrants" and lived on land before adapting to the water. When studying their fins, scientists have found that they are formed like legs and toes. So maybe our closest sea friends were wolf-like land animals once.

29. Dolphins are "opportunistic" feeders, meaning they will eat those fish, squid and crustaceans (such as shrimp) available to them at that time.

30. Dolphins can migrate if their needs of food are not met. Even though they are not migratory animals, they will move to places where they have enough food and the climatic conditions are suitable to their body temperatures.

31. It has been proved by scientists that dolphins give themselves names. They develop their own individual whistles and they recognize theirs and other dolphins' names.

32. Dolphins are divided into two distinct family groups. The larger, more common group is the delphinidae family, which are salt-water dolphins. The smaller group is the Platanistidae family, which are freshwater dolphins.

33. A dolphin's body is made to help them move through the water quickly and without using too much energy. They rely on their pectoral fins and the fluke (tail) to help them navigate their way through the water.

34.. Each day an adult dolphin produces about 4 liters of urine and about 1.4 kilos of feces. Because the volume of fluid produced during each urination episode is small, the urine quickly disperses in the water and is un-noticeable. Feces, on the other hand, usually appear as a cloud of thin green liquid.

35. A bottlenose dolphin's stomach consists of three compartments or chambers. (Most dolphin species have a three-chambered stomach, although there are a few species with only two stomachs).

36. The first chamber, acting as a "storage unit", is responsible for holding swallowed food until the other two chambers are ready to proceed with digestion. In this way a dolphin can rapidly consume large amounts of food.

37. A dolphin's sonar or echolocation is rare in nature and is far superior to either the bat's sonar or human-made sonar.

38. A baby dolphin must learn to hold its breath while nursing.

39. Dolphins are connected to their mothers by an umbilical cord inside a womb, dolphins have belly buttons.

4o. Dolphins don't have a sense of smell, but they do have a sense of taste and, like humans, can distinguish between sweet, sour, bitter, and salty tastes.

41. Some dolphins can dive as deep as 1,500 feet (457.5 m), but they usually stay within 200 to 250 feet (61 to 76.3 m) of the water's surface.

42. Dolphins can move each eye independently. They can move each eye up, down, forward, and backward, giving them nearly 360 degrees of vision.

43. Bottlenose dolphins sleep with one eye open and the other closed.

44. A female bottlenose dolphin squirts milk into the mouth of its calf using muscular contractions.

45. Bottlenose dolphin uses its mouth for eating and nose (blowhole) for communicating.

46. A bottlenose dolphin's outermost skin layer will be replaced every two to four hours to get rid of any algae and bacteria that tend to stick to

the skin. This also reduces the drag and improves the speed.

47. Bottlenose dolphin's eyeballs move independently of each other. They can look ahead and look back at the same time.

48. Bottlenose dolphins are warm-blooded, and their body temperature is about 37 °C (98 °F), which is the same as that of humans.

49. Bottlenose dolphins see quite well both below and above the water.

50. Studies show that dolphins have excellent hearing as well. They can hear frequencies that are least 10 times what the best adult hearing can offer.

51. A dolphin can make about 700 clicking sounds per second. The clicks come from deep inside the dolphin's head, underneath the blowhole.

52. Among the different species of dolphins, life spans range between 12 and 80 years. Bottlenose dolphins live into their 50s, and orcas can live into their 80s. Typically, the bigger the dolphin, the longer the lifespan.

53. Every year, a dolphin's teeth grow a new layer, like the rings inside a tree trunk. Scientists

can tell how old a dolphin is from the layers on its teeth.

54. Dolphins are one of the few animals that can use tools. They use broken sea sponges to protect their noses while they forage for food.

55. Some dolphins can see colors and others can't; some only see in shades of grey, while others see blue-green colors.

56. Bottlenose dolphins are kings of communication! They send each other messages in different ways – they squeak and whistle and use body language, leaping out of the water, snapping their jaws and even butting heads.

57. Dolphins must tell themselves when to breathe; it's not an automatic response like it is for humans.

58. Dolphins have names and respond when called. Dolphins within pods have their own "signature whistle," just like a name, and other dolphins can use that special whistle to get the attention of their pod mates.

59. Dolphins can see with sound, they use their tell-tale clicks which travel long distances and bounce off objects. This allows them to know how far away the object is and the shape, density, movement and texture of it.

60. With echolocation, dolphins can distinguish between a ball that is 2½ inches in diameter and one that is 2¼ inches in diameter.

61. Dolphins can recognize themselves in the mirror, and they love to admire themselves.

62. A two-headed dolphin was found in western Turkey in 2014.

63. Some dolphins can understand as many as 60 words, which can make up 2,000 sentences. They also show signs of self-awareness.

64. Blocking off a dolphin's ears with suction cups hardly affects its hearing, yet if its lower jaw is covered with a rubber jacket, a dolphin will have trouble hearing. This has led scientists to believe sound may be carried from the water to its inner ear through the lower jawbone or even its entire body.

65. A 260-pound dolphin eats approximately 33 pounds of fish daily without gaining weight.

66 Dolphins can kill sharks with their noses. They may even circle around a shark to coordinate an attack.

67. Just a tablespoon of water in a dolphin's lung could drown it, while a human would drown after two tablespoons.

68. If you killed a dolphin during the time of Ancient Greece it was considered sacrilegious and was punishable by death. They Greeks called them "hieros ichthys" which means sacred fish.

69. Number of offspring is usually one calf; twins are rare.

70. A dolphin spends most of its life holding its breath.

71. Dolphins have a complex social structure and seem to have a wide range of emotions, including humor. Large pods can have 1,000 members or more.

72. Pink dolphins, called "botos," are albino dolphins. They typically live in Brazil but have been seen in the Gulf of Mexico.

73. Dolphins and porpoises are related, but they are not the same. Porpoises have smaller heads and shorter snouts than dolphins. They also have spade-shaped teeth, while dolphins have cone-shaped teeth.

74. Dolphins' sonar seems not to detect the fine threads of fishing nets, and millions of dolphins have drowned because of becoming entangled.

75. Some scientists think that dolphins can also use their high-pitched sounds to stun or paralyze fish while hunting.

76. Dolphins cannot swim backward, which makes it difficult for them to escape fishing nets. If they can't get to the surface, they can drown in a matter of minutes.

77. A female dolphin will assist in the birth of another's baby dolphin, and if it is a difficult birth, the "midwife" might help pull out the baby. Other dolphins, including bulls, will swim around the mother during birth to protect her.

78. In 2006, the Yangtze River dolphin was named functionally extinct.

79. The Atlantic spotted dolphin can be found living in warm tropical climates throughout the year and tend to prefer living in and around the coastal waters or around the continental shelf of the Atlantic Ocean.

80. Atlantic spotted dolphins are extremely protective of their young and will help each other to care for them. They also tend to do their best to protect the pregnant females from enemies including sharks.

81. The Atlantic spotted dolphin form groups of about 50 and they are also known to move around with other species of dolphins without any conflicts among them.

82. This can be extremely useful when a mother for instances needs to keep track of one of her kids or when two friends are communicating with one another in a large pod.

83. The Atlantic spotted dolphin is only found in the ocean. They are known to live in a variety of locations including the oceans around the United States, Africa, Europe, the Bahamas, and the Gulf of Mexico.

84. There is a hierarchy among Atlantic spotted dolphin that depends upon many factors including their size, age, and gender.

85. Atlantic spotted dolphin tend to hunt in groups as they have a tactic that allows them to get their prey into a big circle. Then they can come at these schools of fish from all angles.

86. These dolphins enjoy maintaining a high level of social interaction with one another and can often be seen performing leaps and various acrobatic stunts.

7. The average estimated lifespan for these dolphins is believed to be around 30 – 40 years.

88. The Atlantic spotted dolphin matures between the ages of 8 – 15 with most dolphins maturing around 12 years of age.

89. Young Atlantic spotted dolphins are born after a gestation period of 11 or 12 months. They have no spots when they are born. They first

start to develop spots about the time they are weaned. The Atlantic Spotted Dolphin has a life span of around 45 years.

90.Dolphins may bump into one another or visualize their body language by spy hopping or leaping out of the water to alert other dolphins of various interests or threats or to display their physical abilities.

91. Dolphins may bump into one another or visualize their body language by spy hopping or leaping out of the water to alert other dolphins of various interests or threats or to display their physical abilities.

92. Because the Atlantic spotted dolphin can be found near the coastline they are more susceptible to being accidentally harmed by local fisherman while offshore dolphins may face threats by fishing nets and predators such as sharks.

93. It is also capable of diving to up to 60 meters, remaining underwater for up to 6 minutes.

94. The beak of the Atlantic spotted dolphin is long and sharply demarcated from the melon, and the dorsal fin is tall and sickle-shaped.

95. Some dolphin species face the threat of extinction, often directly because of human behavior.

96. When it comes to family orcas are extremely family oriented and as many as four generations of family members may be seen traveling together.

97. Maui's dolphins tend to stay in small pods consisting of 1 – 5 dolphins.

98. It usually takes around 6 months for a baby Maui's dolphin to learn to hunt and be able to feed itself at which point it can stop feeding on its mother's milk.

99. Today Maui dolphins can only be seen living off the North West Coast of the central and upper North Island areas.

100. The dolphin's most dangerous enemy is humans.

Please check this out:

Our other best-selling books for kids are-

Most Popular Animal Quiz book for Kids: 100 amazing animal facts

Quiz Book for Kids: Science, History, Geography, Biology , Computer & Information Technology

English Grammar for Kids: Most Easy Way to learn English Grammar

Solar System & Space Science- Quiz for Kids : What You Know About Solar System

Know about Sharks: 100 Amazing Fun Facts with Pictures

Know About Whales:100+ Amazing & Interesting Fun Facts with Pictures: " Never known Before "- Whales facts

Know About Dinosaurs : 100 Amazing & Interesting Fun Facts with Pictures

Know About Kangaroos: Amazing & Interesting Facts with Pictures

Know About Penguins: 100+ Amazing Penguin Facts with Pictures

Know About Dolphins :100 Amazing Dolphin Facts with Pictures

100 Amazing Quiz Q & A About Penguin: Never Known Before Penguin Facts

English Grammar Practice Book for elementary kids: 1000+ Practice Questions with Answers

Made in United States
North Haven, CT
02 January 2023

30460890R00019